YoungWriters

The BigG
Poetry Machine

Southern Counties

Edited by Aimée Vanstone & Lisa Adlam

First published in Great Britain in 2009 by:

Young Writers
Remus House
Coltsfoot Drive
Peterborough
PE2 9JX
Telephone: 01733 890066
Website: www.youngwriters.co.uk

Book Design by Spencer Hart & Tim Christian

SB ISBN 978-1-84924-015-4

Foreword

Young Writers' Big Green Poetry Machine is a showcase for our nation's most brilliant young poets to share their thoughts, hopes and fears for the planet they call home.

Young Writers was established in 1991 to nurture creativity in our children and young adults, to give them an interest in poetry and an outlet to express themselves. Seeing their work in print will encourage them to keep writing as they grow, and become our poets of tomorrow.

Selecting the poems has been challenging and immensely rewarding. The effort and imagination invested by these young writers makes their poems a pleasure to enjoy reading time and time again.

Contents

Westover Primary School, Copnor

The Poems

Litter

L itter and rubbish, what a disgusting sight,
I t just stays there and it isn't right,
T ake up all your courage, make sure you pick it up,
T hink before you throw, just to make you see,
E veryone together now, it isn't just up to me,
R educe, reuse and recycle, it's the way to be!

Lucas Wong (10)
Bitterne Junior School, Southampton

Rainforest Poem

An eerie whistle in the trees,
Which just makes this once wonderful forest a place of despair
And now the only remains of it are just a whisper in the night.

The dark, murky dunes of the old rainforest make it the ultimate,
Uninpenitrible task for any mortal to survive in,
The dark wasteland of the forest.

Samuel Grundy (9)
Bitterne Junior School, Southampton

The Trees

The trees are ruined, the trees are old,
The trees have already started to mould,
Save the world before its destruction,
Worn out wolves homeless again,
Help these creatures, their homes are destroyed
Because we need paper,
Reuse paper again and again,
Please save the rainforest over again
And save the animals or they will die.

Dante Foster (9)
Bitterne Junior School, Southampton

Rainforest Poem

Sharp, jagged chainsaws cutting down the homes
of delicate animals,
Razor sharp saws cutting down old trees,
Steam rollers flattening down all of the old trees,
Tired animals wildly tumbling around finding new homes each day,
We must stop the rainforest from being destroyed
Or all animals will be killed.

Jay Earp (9)
Bitterne Junior School, Southampton

Untitled

Weak and harmless,
He looks like he is half-dead,
Starving to death,
He has no money.

Adam Robinson (9)
Bitterne Junior School, Southampton

The Homeless Poem

The battered homeless, as battered as a rubber
That has been used and used,
The empty-hearted living, sadly on the street,
As sad as can be,
The worm out homeless lie on the streets,
Sadly the town was left lonely for them to sort out,
The uncomfortable left on the road,
The unforgettable town will never be forgotten.

Mollie Milburn (10)
Bitterne Junior School, Southampton

The RainForest

R ain doesn't stop the loss of trees,
A ll the forest is being cut down,
I n the forest with no trees,
N o homes for animals,
F orests are not remaining,
O ptions are open,
aR e you causing this?
E veryone needs to help,
S oon the forest will not remain,
T rees are saying goodbye.

Jaden Gayle (9)
Bitterne Junior School, Southampton

Rainforest Poem

The battered trees, mangled and weary,
Throwing away homes of animals, leaving animals homeless.

We are making animals deserted from their homes,
Destroyed trees, mangled and mouldy.

Sharp, jagged chainsaws shredding trees into paper,
The more we are cutting down, the more furious we are getting,
Cute animals are being killed because of us,
Unforgettable trees that were homes to the cute animals,
That is soon going to die out if we continue.

Harry Parker (9)
Bitterne Junior School, Southampton

Eco-Friendly

R ecycle to help people,
E arthquakes are terrible,
C rippled homes are not good,
Y ou can help by recycling,
C ars are not good, walk more,
L earn about recycling,
E co-friendly.

Max Cooper (9)
Bitterne Junior School, Southampton

Extinction Poem

E xtinction is disgraceful,
eX ecution of life,
T rees once home to animals,
I hate this disgusting sight,
N ever do it yourself,
C os it ain't right,
T ime's passing by,
I f we don't stop,
O verdose of chopping trees,
N ever to be seen again.

Amelia Jerome (10)
Bitterne Junior School, Southampton

Litter

Stop, stop, stop that litter,
Things are getting bitter,
So let's make things better,
So send a big fat letter,
To the President of the United States!

Aicha Yasmin Kherraz (9)
Bitterne Junior School, Southampton

Recycle

Recycle stuff, keep it going,
To be green, recycle milk bottles, newspapers and paper,
Look at all of the parks, all full of rubbish,
Pick all of it up and put it in the bin,
Be green, please, please, remember,
Reuse,
Reduce
And recycle.

Mitchell Thorn (9)
Bitterne Junior School, Southampton

The Weak Man

Weak and harmless, he looks like he is half-dead,
He looks like a poor and helpless man,
He lives on no food at all and is a very, very lonely man,
Who lives all by himself,
He has nothing at all,
He is very brave in some ways,
He would never go out on the streets like that,
I would be scared.

Amber Folds (9)
Bitterne Junior School, Southampton

Homeless

People walk straight past them,
You should be ashamed,
How do they end up like this?
There must be a way.

No one should do this,
We should stop this now,
Where are their families?

They get their food from a rubbish bin,
Why, oh why, oh why?
They must be hungry,
They may want some food.

Everyone should have a home,
We don't see this every day,
Why should it be this way?
Is he homeless?
Yes he is.

I think we should do something about this,
No one should be like this,
We should stop this,
Now!

Olivia Lloyd (9)
Bitterne Junior School, Southampton

Untitled

Don't waste,
It's a disgrace,
Go to Michael,
He recycles,
I find him where?
Over there,
So people went to Michael,
To learn how to recycle,
What can we recycle?
Paper and card, recycle, recycle,
What else can you recycle?
Glass, paper and metal,
Recycle, I will recycle,
I'll do my best,
Now my room won't be a mess,
Now my people spread the word,
I am off to save the world!

Megan Sunassee-Hepworth (9)
Bitterne Junior School, Southampton

Recycle Me

R ecycle,
E arth is better for picking up rubbish,
C n you save your planet?
Y ou must recycle,
C ars pollute the Earth,
L earn how to recycle,
E limate pollution.

M ake the world safe,
E co rules!

Luke James Smith (9)
Bitterne Junior School, Southampton

Recycle!

Recycle, recycle, now come and save the environment,
It is easy to do,
Help the world, recycle paper, glass, bottles and plastic,
Come and recycle and remember the three 3 R's.
Reuse, reduce and recycle.

Debora Joseph (9)
Bitterne Junior School, Southampton

A Cough And A Cold

A cough and a cold,
Maybe an ear infection,
A cough and a cold,
Not an election,
Everyone look at these people who are alive,
But now they won't be able to strive,
So everyone do stand up for the people who aren't very well,
Otherwise they'll be in Hell,
So please, please help,
Otherwise I will yelp!
Everyone gather round,
They won't make a sound,
Now they are harmless to us and we can help,
They can do things, things like us,
Like going on a bus.

Natasha McIntyre (9)
Bitterne Junior School, Southampton

Homeless

H ungry every day for he has nothing,
And no one O utstanding to see, so many people like this,
M oney is all this poor fellow needs to start afresh,
E very day this man just sits here,
L end some money to this poor man,
E ven the smallest amount of money
could make this man so happy,
S o help this man go back and start again,
S ometimes just think for a couple of seconds
and think what if it was the other way round.

Liam Perress (9)
Bitterne Junior School, Southampton

Timeless

Sad and hungry, cold and bare, this man is homeless,
It's disgraceful and unfair,
He's out on the street, neglected and alone,
Why don't you help him, help give him a home?
It's not too hard, in fact it's quite easy,
Send some money to charity,
Don't feel sad, don't feel guilty,
Help this man, give him a family.

Molly Walton (10)
Bitterne Junior School, Southampton

Rainforest Poem

The destroyed and unforgettable rainforest,
Has been abandoned,
So now a wasteland of battered crumbly Earth,
It is so disappointing for all animals,
An unnatural eerie sound,
Buzzes around like an angry bee,
This magnificent sight has now been swept away,
Like a hurricane destroying houses,
Everyone stop cutting down these amazing exotic rainforests
And animals' homes.

Sam Spiller (9)
Bitterne Junior School, Southampton

The Homeless

The dread of people without a home,
The care of people not being used,
The unkind people ignoring all homeless,
The family crying for help every night,
Stop and think!

Kiah Jeneway (9)
Bitterne Junior School, Southampton

Save The Rainforest

These cruel unforgettable things that people do, shocking sadness,
The tragic careless things that people do are just horrible,
The people whirring chainsaws in action, chopping
down the remaining trees,
As the sadness gathers on this disastrous plain,
It is just a reminder, so think.

Hannah Rudge (9)
Bitterne Junior School, Southampton

Untitled

The unforgettable sight of the hurt man stays with me,
The unfairness fades away in the moonlight as night comes in,
The troubled man disappears from thought,
The harmed man sits until someone comes for him,
The rubbish around him consumes your mind.

Annie Pringle (9)
Bitterne Junior School, Southampton

Recycle

Recycle, recycle,
Don't make mess,
Go to see Michael,
Who recycles,
He's the best,
Don't waste time,
Recycle, recycle,
Do it now,
It's great for the environment,
Save the world,
Recycle, reduce, reuse,
What can we recycle?
Paper, cardboard and plastic,
But remember not plastic bags.

Yasmine Marlow
Bitterne Junior School, Southampton

Rainforest

The old battered stumps of what used to be a
long piece of unforgettable joy,
The worst that could be done has been done,
The ragged chainsaws have done their worst,
It is time to fight off the chainsaw and the men don't care,
We have to take action now and make those men who don't care,
Care!

Callum Button (10)
Bitterne Junior School, Southampton

The Rainforest

The eerie sharp saws cutting down the trees,
The homeless animals are disappointed,
Everyone is shocked to see the rainforests,
All of the trees have been cut down,
The animals have nowhere to go,
Their home has been removed.

Olivia Knight (9)
Bitterne Junior School, Southampton

Rainforest Poem

The rainforest was the home of many animals,
But now all that remains is the mangled tree stumps,
We need to stop cutting down the rainforest trees,
Or it might be too late,
Then it will be harder to breathe.

Gabriel Hindle (9)
Bitterne Junior School, Southampton

Trees

Trees, trees, can't you see,
How important they can be?
They give out air for you and me,
To breathe for life, for life to breathe.

Apple, plum, orange, pear,
Look yum, over there,
Apples as green as grass down low,
Plums as round as basketballs,
Oranges as oval as little red dodgems,
Pears as tall as a house.

Freya Boulton (9)
Colebrook Junior School, Stratton

Tree Valley

Starting with a very small seed,
Pushing through the ground with speed,
Soon the tree begins to show,
Giving shade from head to toe.

With branches long as snakes
And leaves as smooth as silk,
The bark as rough as a garden rake,
Sap as creamy as milk.

Leaves as soft as a pillow,
On the branches of a willow,
Oxygen, food, shade and colour,
Without the trees, life would be duller.

Charlie Emmerson (8)
Colebrook Junior School, Stratton

Please, Please Don't Cut Down The Trees

They give us fruit, they give us life,
They make us live all the time,
So please, please don't cut these trees,
They make us live until we freeze,
They are as tall as skyscrapers,
As wide as mountains,
As rough as sand,
As light as feathers.

Lewis Paul Dickinson (9)
Colebrook Junior School, Stratton

Don't Cut Down Trees

Please, please, I'm on my knees,
Chucking out paper is really a waste,
In the woods, I see people cutting down trees.

Cory Francome (7)
Colebrook Junior School, Stratton

Trees

Don't cut down trees,
We won't be able to breathe.

Chucking out paper is really a waste,
So please, please I'm on my knees,
Don't cut down trees!

Matthew Tilling (7)
Colebrook Junior School, Stratton

Saving A Tree

Starting with a very small seed,
Pushing through the ground with speed,
Soon the tree begins to show,
Giving shade from head to toe.

Leaves are soft as a pillow,
And the branches of a willow,
Giving shade, sun and shower,
The tree grows from power,
Then it starts to rain,
Then the tree grows fruit and veg.

Naomi Mary Anderson (8)
Colebrook Junior School, Stratton

The Birds And Animals

Lovely animals climbing trees
And a very wind day indeed,
Birds are tweeting away in the morning,
To wake us up for school or work.

Courtney Hunt (7)
Colebrook Junior School, Stratton

Where The Apple Tree Once Stood

By my house there stood a tree,
That had lots of fruit that I picked every year,
But then I heard a noise,
And the tree got chopped down,
It took three months.

Alice Edmonds (7)
Colebrook Junior School, Stratton

All About Trees

Please, please, don't cut down trees,
I'm on my knees,
Trees give us air to help us breathe,
Getting paper is just a waste,
Getting furniture is losing all of our oxygen,
They give us life,
They give us fruit,
They give us air for the planet.

Daniel Hulse (8)
Colebrook Junior School, Stratton

Lovely Tree

Lovely tree standing by,
All of a sudden a man comes by,
'Watch out kid,' the man says,
In a croaky voice,
I stand back, *rrrrr!*
The wonderful tree falls down,
'Ow!' I say sadly.

Lois Hill (7)
Colebrook Junior School, Stratton

Untitled

Squirrels, birds and monkeys say
'No, you're killing our homes.'
Branches reaching high, take time to grow,
Birds whistling won't have a home,
Monkeys swinging won't have a tree to swing on,
Squirrels won't have any oak trees to have nuts for dinner,
Do you know trees are important,
Think about it.

Annabelle Cuss (7)
Colebrook Junior School, Stratton

The Big Green Poetry Machine

They give us fruit,
Hey give us life,
They make us live all the time,
So please, please don't cut those trees,
They're as tall as skyscrapers,
They're as rough as sand,
Trees are as wide as mountains,
Their leaves are as light as feathers.

Joshua Rogers (9)
Colebrook Junior School, Stratton

Trees

Starting with a very small seed,
Pushing through the ground with speed,
Soon the tree begins to show,
Giving shade from head to toe.

Leaves as soft as a pillow,
On the branches of a willow,
Oxygen, food, shade and colour,
Without the trees, life would be duller.

The trees as tall as towers,
Leaves as crunchy as cornflakes,
Trunks as strong as walls,
Branches as long as snakes.

Leah Waters (7)
Colebrook Junior School, Stratton

Water

Streams trickle as the source comes into sight,
Rivers gush as they reach the angry sea like a hungry
hyena in a field of bison,
Waves snarl as they tumble down to the fearsome boulders,
Typhoons howl in the midnight sky,
Oceans lying on the seabed, like a worn out dog resting his head,
So where would we be without water?
I think I know, do you?

Sam Guyatt (10)
Colebrook Junior School, Stratton

Water

The ocean consumed the landscape,
The thunderous flood gushed through the doorway,
Waves sneezed onto the top of the cliffs,
The waterfall licked stones on its way,
The sea howled like a hungry dog,
Water diving into the ocean like a diver,
Water leaping over the stones like a kangaroo,
The pond whispered on small puddles,
The rain dripped in the puddles,
Then we consumed water.

Sophie Boycott (9)
Colebrook Junior School, Stratton

Moving Water

Waves like a hungry lion pouncing on its prey,
Raindrops dribbling like a baby teething,
Rivers rushing like a mum wanting to get in and
Out of the supermarket,
Puddles like a dog sleeping,
Ponds whisper like children in class,
Waterfalls like a person diving,
Sea consuming the beach,
Without water nothing would live.

Jessica Williams (10)
Colebrook Junior School, Stratton

The Sea Beast

The sea crashing and tumbling on the sandy shores,
Like a malevolent tiger ripping the meat off its prey,
The sea is a starving lion consuming the beach bit by bit,
The sea is an angry little child tossing the boat around
as if it was a ball,

The sea is a feline,
Scratching away at the cliff,
The sea is a python pouncing on its dinner.

Water can harm but heal at the same time.

Nathan Harvey Allpress (10)
Colebrook Junior School, Stratton

Water

Oceans sneezed as loud as a hyena barking,
A wave licked the sandy beach as if it was a lollipop
The colour of a rainbow,
Waterfalls howled as the golden sun crept down behind the hills,
Swimming pools slowly moved like a robber,
Seas danced like a tap dancer in the moonlight,
Ponds all around the world jumped onto the moon
Because of a tornado,
Rivers everywhere dived as if they were at the Olympics,
The puddle leapt as if he was a frog,
Monsoons demanded the attention of the village,
Lakes run around the world,
Rain sang as the storm passed by,
Don't forget water keeps the Earth alive.

Laura Neilan (10)
Colebrook Junior School, Stratton

Our World Of Water

Drops of water dance in the sink like little ballerinas,
The puddle swirls violently like an angry whirlpool,
Mini drops of water dive down as the shower's turned on,
Drops of rain shower the Earth like a child's tears,
Streams slowly drift towards the trees,
The lake swims over the stones rapidly,
As the ocean consumes the beach,
The waterfall plunges into the turquoise lake,
Like a giant hosepipe.

Lauren Waters (10)
Colebrook Junior School, Stratton

Water's Movement

Oceans whisper,
Drips dance,
Splashes snarl,
Waterfalls lick the grey ragged rocks,
Waves sneeze,
Rain trickles,
Lakes toss,
Puddles are calm on the ground,
Drops rush,
Ponds swirl,
Tsunamis jump,
Streams howl on cold, windy, winter's night,
Water is keeping the world alive.

Emily Kingsman (10)
Colebrook Junior School, Stratton

Water

Dripping from rooftops,
Gushing down into streams,
Waves pounce like lions reaching for their prey,
Why are we wasting it when it's vital to all of us?
Act now, stop wasting water.

Josie May McAteer (9)
Colebrook Junior School, Stratton

Water

A drip of water pounces into the sewers near the drain,
It stalks into a path followed by rain,
Soon the rain rages like a shower,
Going into the ocean with so much power,
Later the ocean licks the rocks,
While a drip goes to the docks,
The ocean soon turns into a thunderous flood,
Growing all the plants out of their bud,
The flood soon consumes all of the land,
Stretching like a rubber band,
We shall tame water on our planet,
So then it can't destroy our world . . . can it?

Charlie Humphreys (9)
Colebrook Junior School, Stratton

Water Is The Best!

Waterfall sneezed as it crashes against the lake,
Water hurdling over the rocks, like a javelin in Olympics.

Water gushes through the lake escaping to the sea,
Waves howl as they crash against the sand,
Waves pouncing to the surface, like a hungry dog.

A shower of tears consumes the planet as raindrops fall,
Rain rages down crashing against the floor,
Like a bomb falling from the sky.

We will not live without water.

Jack Skyrme (10)
Colebrook Junior School, Stratton

Water

Raindrops trickle down the rooftops,
Rivers racing down to a swirling lake,
Waterfalls dive into gushing streams,
Sea gargles down the swirling of the whirlpool,
Ocean waves pounce like a lion leaping for its prey.

Water is a crucial part of the Earth and what would we do without it?

Alice Telling (9)
Colebrook Junior School, Stratton

Water

River leaps onto the banks like a lion pouncing on his prey,
Waterfalls trickle over the cliffside into the raging sea,
Waves snarl as they tumble down to the shore,
Rain gushes down from the clouds as it consumes the town,
We need water to live.

Will Clarke (10)
Colebrook Junior School, Stratton

Help The Planet

Help the planet by no pollution,
Stop throwing litter around,
Try and make a start,
Just try to help,
Or our planet will be destroyed.

Victoria Emmerson (11)
Colebrook Junior School, Stratton

Water

The beautiful clear water pouncing over the mossy rocks,
Look at the flow, face and slow.

Look at the rain twisting and turning like butter churning.

Look at the waves splishing and splashing,
Like a light bulb smashing.

Jake Cox (10)
Colebrook Junior School, Stratton

Water

My river is a bloodstream,
Running through my body,
My tears are like raindrops,
Falling from the sky,
My throat is a well,
Swallowing saliva,
My stomach is an ocean swirling around,
My eyes are the whirlpools going round,
Don't waste water, there are people
Who need it more than us.

Harvey Ritchie (10)
Colebrook Junior School, Stratton

Water

Waves licking and sneezing in the ocean,
Rain dripping like the tap running wild,
Waves smashing like a whale leaping,
Sea gusting against the rock,
Waterfall creeping down the bank side,
Showers gusting like waterfalls smashing,
Oceans creeping like a shark hunting,
Bath running like a short painting,
The river dancing in the bank side,
The countryside needs water.

Christopher Rogers (11)
Colebrook Junior School, Stratton

Water Around Us

Water, dancing drops,
Water, trickling through my toes,
Water, streams sneezing,
Water, rain racing,
Water, like a man diving,
Water, gushing, gurgling,
Water, sea skipping,
Water, lakes leaping,
Waves, like a pounding lion,
Waterfall, winding its way,
Water, consuming everything in his path,
Water quenches fire,
Water, nothing can live without it,
Water, bringing life to Earth.

Eleanor Dixon (9)
Colebrook Junior School, Stratton

Litter

Mess maker,
Animal trapper,
Fire starter,
Not environmentally friendly,
Put it in bins,
Don't throw it on the floor,
Just keep it clean!

Calum Hunt & Carl Edwards
Colebrook Junior School, Stratton

Animals

A world with no animals,
N o more tree chopping,
I magine you're an animal shedding a tear,
M eat, fur and skin - do not hunt,
A nimal extinction is near,
L et wildlife live,
S ave our animals.

Tamzin Meads & Harrison Wallage (9)
Colebrook Junior School, Stratton

Recycle Your Rubbish

L itter is messy,
I t makes a horrible smell,
T o stop littering, put your rubbish in the bin,
T ry to stop polluting,
E njoy Earth without litter,
R ecycle your rubbish.

Thomas Matthews (9)
Colebrook Junior School, Stratton

Litter

Drink me,
Don't discard me,
Squash me flat,
Throw me in the bin,
Tip me in the truck,
Take me to the recycling plant,
Make me into a new metal can.

Bethany Jackson
Colebrook Junior School, Stratton

In Danger Of Extinction

Stop cutting,
Stop chopping,
Stop slicing the trees,
Make extinction end,
Birds dying,
Monkeys falling,
Imagine dying,
Stop cutting.

Laurie Hill (9)
Colebrook Junior School, Stratton

Animals

Animals are dying,
Some tall, some small,
Some wide, some thin,
It's a dreadful sin,
All the wild cats,
Many singing birds,
Wildlife is in danger,
Stop the extinction.

Courtney Gerrard (9)
Colebrook Junior School, Stratton

Recycling

Different boxes to put me in,
Then I go through a big machine,
It makes me good and clean,
With a lot of steam,
Soon I will be in the shops with my friends,
Or at home in your fridge.

Loren McAlpine (9)
Colebrook Junior School, Stratton

Rainforest

R ainforest disappearing,
A nimals with no homes,
I nside the forest animals are dying,
N o food in the forest,
F orests being cut down,
O rang-utans with no homes,
R escuing species,
E arth exposed,
S potty leopards and monkeys with no home,
T rying to find another home.

Connor Michael Gerrard (9)
Colebrook Junior School, Stratton

War

Guns shooting,
People dying,
They should get on,
It's life threatening,
It's just wrong,
Just stop!

Erika Leigh Tovell (9)
Colebrook Junior School, Stratton

Nature

N ever harm the environment,
A lways put litter in the bin,
T hings might die,
U nkind to nature,
R ubbish on the floor, so pick it up,
E arth might never be the same if you don't help.

Joseph Cuss
Colebrook Junior School, Stratton

Poverty

Poverty all around,
Poor people suffering
On the ground,
Help poverty to stop!
People are dying,
No money,
No clothes,
No homes,
Community is suffering,
Help it stop!

Sophie Mary Bull (9)
Colebrook Junior School, Stratton

War Of The World

Battle tantrums,
Country riot,
Weapon users,
Guns shooting,
People killing,
It's horrid . . .
Stop!

Jana Karin Runziman
Colebrook Junior School, Stratton

No More War

No more fighting,
No more hurting people,
No more people crying,
No more people trying to hide,
No more homes destroyed,
No more war.

Liam Iles (9)
Colebrook Junior School, Stratton

The Diary Of A Rainforest Tree

On Monday, a great giant waxy monkey frog
Was hopping from a cracked branch to another one,
On Tuesday, lovely bright tropical coloured parrots,
Were sitting in the high canopy above,
Squawking as loud as they could,
On Wednesday, black and gold toucans nested in
Humungous holes in the high top of the trees,
Holes as big as a head,
On Thursday, dotty jaguars growled and tried to climb the tree,
On Friday, a growling chainsaw loomed straight into the tree
To snap it down,
On Saturday, men shaved bark and men took the leftover wood
Somewhere else.
On Sunday, a black, greyish, dark, bare and cold space
Was quite big.

Shannon Fortune (9)
Colebrook Junior School, Stratton

The Diary Of A Rainforest Tree

On Monday, graceful birds flew beautifully,
On Tuesday, a red-ruffed lemur sneakily spied on the other animals,
On Wednesday, a baby squirrel monkey tried to swing on the vines,
On Thursday, a chameleon slowly climbed the tree,
On Friday, a growling chainsaw powerfully hit into the tree,
On Saturday, a humungous monster truck came and loaded the tree,
On Sunday, a space, no tree, no animals.

Destiny Keville (8)
Colebrook Junior School, Stratton

The Diary Of A Rainforest

On Monday lots of beautiful branches of parrots,
On Tuesday, a black and white bear leapt onto twirly twigs,
On Wednesday, a bird cheeped cheerfully flying,
On Thursday, leaf cutter ants scuttled along,
On Friday, the people cut the old sad tree down,
On Saturday, a big scary lorry took it away,
On Sunday, the poor animals were homeless.

Jessica Legg (7)
Colebrook Junior School, Stratton

The Diary Of A Rainforest Tree

On Monday, a toucan flew to the canopy
Then it started squawking very loudly,
On Tuesday, a red-eyed tree frog was croaking in a rhythm,
On Wednesday, a leopard was growling while stalking its prey,
On Thursday, a three-toed sloth came climbing up the trunk,
On Friday, the tree was cut down and chopped up,
On Saturday, the tree was burnt on a fire,
On Sunday, the tree was ash, nothing but ash.

Sam Crocker (8)
Colebrook Junior School, Stratton

The Diary Of A Rainforest Tree

On Monday, rainbow-coloured parrots perched in a canopy
squawking loudly.
On Tuesday, the pretty red ruby monkey swung from
branch to branch,
On Wednesday, a three-toed sloth climbed the thick trunk,
On Thursday, leaf cutter ants scattered across the rough thick trunk,
On Friday, a ginormous crane cut down the tree,
On Saturday, the log, lazy lays down and goes rotten,
On Sunday, no tree, no home.

Amy Puffett (8)
Colebrook Junior School, Stratton

The Diary Of A Rainforest Tree

On Monday, a multicoloured parrot perched down and
Squawked as loud as could be,
On Tuesday, a crimson howler monkey howled as loudly as ever,
On Wednesday, a three-toed sloth clambered up and up,
As slowly as could be,
On Thursday, a typical family of leaf cutter ants tore at
Emerald leaves,
On Friday, a powerful chainsaw chewed through
The defenceless trunk,
On Saturday, the log, lay silent on the back,
While the black truck took it away,
On Sunday, ash piled onto an empty space as black as smoke.

Alexander Knowles (8)
Colebrook Junior School, Stratton

The Diary Of A Rainforest Tree

On Monday, a bronze-coloured three-toed sloth
Climbed moderately up the tree,
On Tuesday, vivid parrots flew beautifully on the canopy,
Eating nuts and seeds,
On Wednesday, a ginger and milky tiger growled
As the animals tried to pounce on them,
On Thursday, an apricot fox was eating crimson berries off the tree,
On Friday, the woodcutter was cutting the trees down,
On Saturday, the lorries took them away,
On Sunday, they burn it for Bonfire night.

Sharonpreet Kang (8)
Colebrook Junior School, Stratton

Rainforest Poem

On Monday, rainbow-coloured parrots perched on the branches
And squawked loudly,
On Tuesday, chocolate monkeys swung vine to vine,
On Wednesday, leaf cutter ants scurried across the branch,
On Thursday, leaf cutter ants nibbled away the leaves,
On Friday, chainsaws bit through the trunk and growled,
On Saturday, a black growling lorry took it away,
On Sunday, no tree animals, homeless, a big space . . . bare!

Jamie Gibbs (8)
Colebrook Junior School, Stratton

The Diary Of A Rainforest Tree

On Monday, lavender parrots squawked loudly,
On Tuesday, crimson monkeys were looking for food,
On Wednesday, three-toed sloths came climbing up
the canopy branches slowly,
On Thursday, leaf cutter ants were running up and down,
On Friday, somebody came to cut up the trunk,
On Saturday, a lorry came to pick up the tree,
On Sunday, animals had nowhere to live,
They were homeless . . .

Kelly Iles (8)
Colebrook Junior School, Stratton

The Diary Of A Rainforest Tree

On Monday, rainbow-coloured parrots
Glide around the leafy canopy.

On Tuesday, bright red howler monkeys noisily
Swing from branch to branch.

On Wednesday, emerald tree snakes slithered up the lumpy trunks.

On Thursday, black spotted jaguars sneak around
The roots ready to pounce.

On Friday, leaf cutter ants scurry along the forest floor
Carrying their load.

On Saturday, a powerful chainsaw chops it down,
It crashes to the ground.

On Sunday, the sad, homeless animals start to look
For somewhere else to live.

Amie Dumbelton (7)
Colebrook Junior School, Stratton

The Diary Of A Rainforest Tree

On Monday, rainbow-coloured parrots glide around
Their leafy canopy.
On Tuesday, bright red howler monkeys noisily swing
From branch to branch.
On Wednesday, emerald tree snakes slither up its trunk.
On Thursday, black spotted jaguars sneak around its roots,
Ready to pounce.
On Friday, teams of leaf cutter ants scurry along the forest floor,
Carrying their load.
On Saturday, a powerful chainsaw chops it down
And it crashes to the ground.
On Sunday, the sad, homeless animals start to look
For somewhere else to live.

Britanny Matthews (8)
Colebrook Junior School, Stratton

A Diary Of A Rainforest Poem

On Monday, some tropical-coloured parrots perched on the canopy,
Squawking at the top of their voices.

On Tuesday, a scarlet howler monkey
Swung through the emerald leaves.

On Wednesday, a three-toed sloth slowly clambered up the trunk.

On Thursday, I saw one single dart frog,
Hopping up and down.

On Friday, someone threw their lighter on the floor
And burnt the tree down.

On Saturday, ash blew everywhere.

On Sunday, animals died and someone came to clean it all up
With a dustpan and brush.

Lydia Guyatt (7)
Colebrook Junior School, Stratton

A Diary Of A Tree

On Monday, rainbow-coloured parrots sat on a lovely brown branch,
Eating a piece of fruit.

On Tuesday, chocolate coloured spider monkeys
Swung from branch to branch.

On Wednesday, a three-toed sloth climbed up a lovely old tree.

On Thursday, leaf cutter ants scuttled across the hard, bumpy bark.

On Friday, the sound of a horrible chainsaw killing a beautiful tree.

On Saturday, a big, colourful, terrible monster truck
Took the tree away.

On Sunday, a bare silent space appeared and
We never saw that tree again!

Ellie Armishaw (8)
Colebrook Junior School, Stratton

A Fine, Pleasant World

I have a dream,
That the grass will gleam,
And the birds will sing in harmony,
With the whispering of the gentle summer wind.

The world will be free of pollution,
And oil won't be spilt in the ocean,
A new energy source will be found,
And polar bears will no longer drown.

Criminals won't fight,
And everyone will know what's right,
There will be poverty, no more,
Disease, no more,
Poaching won't have taken place,
Cutting down rainforests won't have taken place.

The ice caps won't melt
And we will have felt,
If my dream is reality -
A fine, pleasant world!

Michael Harsley (9)
Corsham Primary School, Corsham

AIDS

Loving fathers, loving mums, loving families have all gone.

Worse than colds, worse than coughs, even worse than cancer!

It goes around killing loads, no one can outlive it.

Mostly the poor and unfortunate get the disease.

Every minute people come and go in Africa.

You never know who will die next!

Shannon White (10)
Heathfield Junior School, Sholing

War

F ighting in Iraq is worse than ever,
I raq is a battle zone, where people are dying,
G renades are planted all in the city, people are getting blown to bits,
H and guns are killing people day by day,
T anks are destroying homes and precious lives,
I n City Central, it used to be a very busy place,
now it's a ghost town,
N utrition is running low, British souls are getting starved,
G as bombs are blowing, soldiers are dying because of this.

Jay-Owen Tudor (10)
Heathfield Junior School, Sholing

War

War is bloody,
War is muddy,
Fighting for blood and
Fighting for glory,
Blood of the brave and,
Set in graves,
War must end,
It must end now,
War is danger and
War is darkness.

Zachary Barnes (10)
Heathfield Junior School, Sholing

Green Trees

T ry not to leave rubbish around,
R ecycle everything,
E co-friendly,
E nvironmentally kind,
S ave our trees!

Harry Lewis (8)
Leehurst Swan School, Salisbury

Trees

Trees are wonderful,
They swish and make a lovely sound,
You just want to sit beneath them
And feel their lovely calm.

But! Cars are making pollution,
Planting trees could be the solution,
Producing oxygen and keeping us alive,
Plant more trees and help us survive.

Henry Palmer (7)
Leehurst Swan School, Salisbury

Rivers

Rives are the nicest thing in the world,
Rivers keep wildlife living,
In the rivers, please God,
Help our rivers to survive in the world,
It is the only way to survive,
Animals need a home.

Sam Kielty-White (8)
Leehurst Swan School, Salisbury

Rules For Paradise

Don't scare the wildlife, it's not nice,
Don't litter on the mountain, it should be paradise,
Do your bit for the environment,
Recycle is our part,
Let's care about the world, it's time to be smart.

Jonathan Mitchell (7)
Leehurst Swan School, Salisbury

Litter

R educe, reuse, recycle,
E veryone should do these things,
C ans drop from hands,
Y es I do it too,
C ans drift down the road,
L itter should be recycled,
E veryone could do their bit.

Marcus Burgess (8)
Leehurst Swan School, Salisbury

Turtles

T urtles are in danger,
U are killing them with nets,
R espect turtles,
T urtles are dying because of people,
L ove turtles,
E ating turtles must be banned,
S wimming turtles is what we want to see!

Max Humphreys (8)
Leehurst Swan School, Salisbury

The Ice Caps

The polar bears live on the ice caps,
We waste our water through dripping taps.

The ice is as slippery as seaweed,
The bears' homes are being spoilt by our greed.

If we walk to school,
The ice will stay really cool.

The polar bears will keep their home
And across the ice they can roam.

Oliver Adams (8)
Leehurst Swan School, Salisbury

Why Here?

Rubbish,
Crying silently,
Swooping seagulls sway overhead,
I ask only one thing . . . why?
Why here?

Hollie Andrews (10)
St Lawrence CE Primary School, Hurstpierpoint

The Rubbish Dump

The big scary tip,
A big dump not to mess with,
As sharp as a knife,
Much bigger than a blue whale
And scarier than a shark.

Reece-Alexander Penn (10)
St Lawrence CE Primary School, Hurstpierpoint

Rubbish

This place smells a lot,
All I see is grey rubbish,
Rubbish everywhere,
All seagulls swoop down at me,
When will this stop happening?

Kathryn Jeffery (11)
St Lawrence CE Primary School, Hurstpierpoint

The Broken Beer Bottle · Haiku

Shattered in pieces,
Broken in bits on the floor,
Laying forever.

Roseanna Leach (10)
St Lawrence CE Primary School, Hurstpierpoint

Foul Junk · Cinquain

Foul junk,
Mounds of rubbish,
Scavenging seagulls choke,
Helpless rubbish lies on its own,
Foul junk!

Fiona Gillespie (11)
St Lawrence CE Primary School, Hurstpierpoint

Foul Junk · Cinquain

Foul junk,
All that I see,
Damp food waste, ancient glass,
Why do people treat me like this?
Help me!

Laura Loutit (10)
St Lawrence CE Primary School, Hurstpierpoint

The Feeling Of A Rubbish Dump · Cinquain

I'm squashed,
Shocked and angry,
Foul, salty, fishy smells,
Cans and glass being chucked at me,
I'm shocked.

Maisie Dadswell (10)
St Lawrence CE Primary School, Hurstpierpoint

Dump Yard · Haiku

Abandoned debris,
Makes a foul stench in the yard,
Man, recycle please.

Freddie Nehls (10)
St Lawrence CE Primary School, Hurstpierpoint

Poem About World Pollution - Haiku

Men are always men,
Surrounded by pollution,
I am almost dead.

Gus Upton (10)
St Lawrence CE Primary School, Hurstpierpoint

Grow Your Own Veg

Grow your own veg,
Because they're really great,
Some are really dry
And some even makes you cry.

Grow your own veg,
Because they're really nice,
It doesn't ever matter if you have it with rice.

Grow your own veg,
Because they're really healthy,
Some make you strong and some even pong.

Kieran Wilkinson (9)
St Lawrence CE Primary School, Hurstpierpoint

Autumn Time!

A utumn leaves are orange, red and yellow,
U nder the trees live many mice and rabbits,
T rees start curling like witches fingers,
U p in the sky, it starts getting darker,
M ammals hide in the ground and trees ready for winter,
N ext month will be winter.

T rees are looking like big sticks,
R ose petals drop to the floor like dead people,
E ggs shiver in the cold,
E xcited children get ready to see flowers,
S now is falling, time to pick the crop, ready to eat.

Alice Bulled (9)
St Lawrence CE Primary School, Hurstpierpoint

Light - Haiku

Turn the lights off now,
Please do not waste energy,
Take care of our world!

Matilda Jones (8)
St Lawrence CE Primary School, Hurstpierpoint

Recycling · Haiku

Here is a message,
Reuse, recycle things now,
For future children.

Josh Hawkins (8)
St Lawrence CE Primary School, Hurstpierpoint

Haiku

Guard our dying world,
Please save precious energy,
Reduce rubbish now.

Arthur Simpkin (8)
St Lawrence CE Primary School, Hurstpierpoint

Have You Thought ...? · Haiku

Have you thought about
Reusing your old rubbish,
To make other things?

Jai Worthington (8)
St Lawrence CE Primary School, Hurstpierpoint

Untitled · Haiku

Saving is too fun,
Recycling helps everyone,
Be cool . . . be green now!

Barney Dunnett (8)
St Lawrence CE Primary School, Hurstpierpoint

Recycle · Haiku

Compost rich and brown,
Sinks into the planet land,
Gorgeous, green garden!

Lloyd Stevens (8)
St Lawrence CE Primary School, Hurstpierpoint

Eco Haiku

Stop, think, reuse now,
You could make a difference,
Take care of our world.

Stop global warming,
Do all you can to help out,
Stop driving your car.

Every day counts,
Help save our dying planet,
Make your difference.

Billy Twigge-Molecey (8)
St Lawrence CE Primary School, Hurstpierpoint

Recycling · Haiku

Here is a message,
Reduce, reuse, recycle,
Take care and think now!

Nicola Burrows (9)
St Lawrence CE Primary School, Hurstpierpoint

Recycling - Haiku

Please recycle now,
Stop wasting energy, kids,
Keep all of us safe.

Hayley Penn (8)
St Lawrence CE Primary School, Hurstpierpoint

Our Environment

L itter is smelly,
I think it's gross,
T o pollute the lovely world,
T o trash the lovely things,
E nvironment and flowers you can recycle them,
R ecycle paper, wood and plastic.

Isabel Hughes (7)
St Lawrence CE Primary School, Hurstpierpoint

Green Day

L ook after the environment,
I don't drop litter,
T ry to recycle your plastic bags,
T ry to recycle your paper,
E asy to recycle your litter,
R ecycle instead!

Jessica Wickes (8)
St Lawrence CE Primary School, Hurstpierpoint

Litter - Cinquain

Litter,
Litter is bad,
Do not litter at all,
When you litter, it is naughty,
Litter.

David Burrows (7)
St Lawrence CE Primary School, Hurstpierpoint

Untitled

Stop the polluting!
Turn off the telly,
Don't leave it on standby,
That's how you save the world!

William Stafford (7)
St Lawrence CE Primary School, Hurstpierpoint

Recycling

R ecycle it now please,
U se it twice if you can,
B ins are useful,
B ut you should put it in the recycling,
I f you are sensible and have a brain,
S top damaging our precious planet,
H old the wasting please!

Millie Peel-Yates (8)
St Lawrence CE Primary School, Hurstpierpoint

Haiku

Put rubbish away,
Recycle like mad always,
Everybody help!

Poppy Haward (7)
St Lawrence CE Primary School, Hurstpierpoint

Untitled

No car, walk or run,
The environment is great,
Be eco-friendly.

Olivia Haskell (7)
St Lawrence CE Primary School, Hurstpierpoint

Plane, Plane Stay On The Ground

Plane, plane, don't fly around,
Plane, plane, don't complain,
Plane, plane, don't make me say it again,
Plane, plane, listen again,
Plane, plane, I'll say it again.

Plane, plane, here we go again,
Plane, plane, don't pollute again,
Plane, plane, stop again,
Plane, plane, don't fly again.

Chris Hill (7)
St Lawrence CE Primary School, Hurstpierpoint

Help The Homeless

The homeless are weak,
They have nothing to eat,
They are everywhere,
Crying in despair,
They have nothing at all,
They can hardly crawl,
Cos there's nothing to do,
But beg for food.

They can never sleep,
Not a crumb to eat,
Not a single penny
And the rich have so many,
No warmth, just cold,
Just a blanket so old,
Homeless people can't walk,
They can barely talk.

Coughs and sneezes,
They have many diseases,
No one seems to care,
No one ever dares,
To go anywhere near them,
They are so condemned,
No cosy bed,
Just the ground instead.

Just a bit of money,
Or say something funny,
A tin of food,
Will change their mood,
Get them on their feet,
Give them something to eat,
Help the homeless,
And stop this mess.

Sarah Parsons (11)
Springhill RC Primary School, Southampton

Destruction Of Rainforests

Chainsaws shouted like heavy machine guns,
The trees started to cry.

The remains of the crisp green leaves were fading,
The trees smashed to the ground.

The wind screamed through the desperate rainforest,
The trees bellowed out for help.

The animals scampered around like autumn leaves
On a blustery day.

I saw the crystal clear water dripping off the sad leaves,
As they were crying salty tears.

Their life was gone, now they would not be so tall,
The bark of the long lost trees was like crocodile skin,
thick and lumpy.

Please fight for these trees today or our world will
Turn into an empty grey nothingness.

Edward Moloney (10)
Springhill RC Primary School, Southampton

Homeless

Homeless people can't survive in the outside world,
They're outside in the freezing cold dying,
Trying to steal from the shops because they have no money,
Have no family, need to be saved before suffering,
Just sitting down in the streets, watching happy families walk by,
They wish they could have a life like the happy families.

We can help them today, any day,
By giving money to the charity and the charity will give
The homeless the money.

So please help today.

Kelly Sousa (10)
Springhill RC Primary School, Southampton

The Homeless

The homeless are weak,
They've nothing to do,
They die of hunger and pollution we do,
So how can we help?
By stopping ourselves,
But if we do we'll be living by ourselves.

They're full of love,
They just need someone to give it to,
So we need to help,
So they don't die too.

They steal to survive,
But we think that's bad,
But they need it to survive,
They need food,
Or else they'll die.

By littering and polluting,
They die a lot quicker,
So we need to stop all this stuff,
So they can get better.

But if we are bad,
Then they get worse
And if we are cruel,
Then they are worse.

We can do,
A lot better to save them,
But if we carry on,
Then we have to save them.

There is no difference between us and them,
So why are they treated with no respect?

Ismaile Khan (10)
Springhill RC Primary School, Southampton

Conflict

C ries over loved ones, the world is not listening,
O ut of the thick, grey smoke, came injured soldiers,
N othing can stop this war, now it has started,
F ears of soldiers murdered in their sleep,
L ost screams wondered in the dark night,
I ncapable of moving, the soldiers wounds eat at their skin,
C ould we stop this horrible war?
T ime is running out, could we ever live in peace?

Reuben McDevitt (10)
Springhill RC Primary School, Southampton

Help The Homeless

Help the homeless,
They need a home,
No food, no drink, no warmth,
Tins of food will make them feel less hungry,
A tin of food will make them happy,
But a home is even better.

Help stop extinction,
More and more animals are dying because of hunters,
Rare animals are dying,
And we need to help them,
People are depressed and it is depressing seeing them dead.

Stop war in Iraq and Afghanistan,
Because it's horrible.

Stop chopping down trees, you're killing the animals
And we're losing oxygen,
Stop cutting down the trees,
Everybody's losing, please.

Megan Doherty (11)
Springhill RC Primary School, Southampton

We Shouldn't Fight

Pointless war scars our Earth,
Humans die on unholy turf,
How can any human wound?
Causing men to be entombed.

Tall or small, old or young,
Black or white, we shouldn't fight!

Death in war is death most foul,
Yet armies fight and soldiers howl,
Cannons rage and bullets storm,
Warriors of love scream and fall.

Tall or small, old or young,
Black or white, we shouldn't fight.

When we hear of war and hate,
Our bodies stop and radiate,
We cry and scream and yell, and roar,
'Stop all the hateful war!'

Tall or small, old or young,
Black or white, we shouldn't fight!

If we all stick together war will leave,
Love is good, so let's live in peace,
Those who hate will be forgiven
And they can join our fantastic living!

Daniel Strickland (10)
Springhill RC Primary School, Southampton

War

War is petrifying, it kills people, it kills people,
War is threatening, it makes people hate and kill,
War is full of conspicuous soldiers,
They are a swarm of bees, with guns as gigantic as trees,
War makes you pay prices by your blood and wounds.

How can someone kill?
The loud screams of horror still echoes in the place,
The ghostly spirit of war will try to make you hate,
But if you were peaceful, then you will not fight.

I think that death by a bullet is the death most foul,
But if there's no war, then the sun will shine
On the sea, making it glitter,
The gorgeous snow white horse shaped clouds
Will gallop across the sapphire blue sky.

Lakshay Nayyar (11)
Springhill RC Primary School, Southampton

Homeless In Need

H aven't got a house,
O ur help means much to them,
M ay die sooner or later,
E arn no money,
L ove and care is what they need,
E ven you can help,
S teal to survive,
S orrow can be seen in their faces.

If we give five pennies a week to charity,
Everything may change,
They won't be called homeless any more,
Because they will have somewhere to live
And food to spare.

Wiktoria Sieradzka (10)
Springhill RC Primary School, Southampton

Racism

R acism is an appalling, horrible thing to do,
A ngry feelings going through your blood-red heart,
C reed, colour of skin doesn't matter,
I f you ever see racism in action, you should call for help,
S haking with fear, trembling like a rattlesnake's back,
M aybe you can be the one to *stop* racism and help.

Kasia Golab (11)
Springhill RC Primary School, Southampton

The Homeless

The homeless are weak
It's hard for them to speak
They live under driving rain
They steal to survive
They sob for help
They are shown no love
They die of hunger.

I think it's unfair
What these people are going through
The children are lonely and oh, so upset
They have nowhere to play
No food to eat and they despair
But what can we do
To get things right?

Help us to help them
To stop begging on the streets
And by giving them shelter
They will die if we don't help them
They are being unjustly punished
Make this your choice
To help the homeless.

Bessem Fon Ngwei (10)
Springhill RC Primary School, Southampton

Making The World A Better Place

They were going to get me,
Bullied, unloved, upset,
I knew they were,
Right behind me,
Laughing, teasing,
I didn't know what to do,
I have this black cloud following me every day.

Playtime starts,
I hate that,
I hide behind the biggest tree,
Trying not to be beaten,
Today a girl came up to me,
Took my hand and said,
'Do you want to be my friend?'
I smiled,
The black cloud disappeared
And the sun came out.

Rayne Alasah (7)
Springhill RC Primary School, Southampton

Making The World A Better Place

Maggie lonely every day,
Teased and taunted every day,
Crouched in a corner every day,
A black cloud floats above her head,
I come up to her, shake her hand,
Pick her up and become her friend,
The black cloud drifts away and
A smile appears on her face,
The sun finally shines above her head.

Sherlyn Sherwin (7)
Springhill RC Primary School, Southampton

Making The World A Better Place

Eley, the useless one,
Eley, the sad one,
Eley, the unhappy one,
Eley, small and hated,
I take her hand and smile,
The sun peeps out winking at her,
She knows now everything is OK.

Madeline Doyle (7)
Springhill RC Primary School, Southampton

Making The World A Better Place

Alice woke with a black cloud above her,
Feeling lonely, Alice walks to school,
Alice hides in the bushes hoping no one sees her,
Feeling unloved every day,
Feeling unwanted every day,
Feeling upset every day,
I take her hands and smile,
She smiles back,
The sun peeps through the clouds,
Alice knows everything is going to change for the better.

Alvina Tom (7)
Springhill RC Primary School, Southampton

Making The World A Better Place

Joshua, upset every day,
Joshua, in agony every day,
Joshua, battered every day,
Joshua, bleeding every day,
Joshua, feeling useless every day,
Joshua, left out every day,
He says, 'Please can I be friends with you?'
I say, 'OK'
Joshua smiles and takes my hand.

Shannon Fisher (7)
Springhill RC Primary School, Southampton

Making The World A Better Place

Ben was unhappy every day,
Ben was left out,
Ben was attacked every day,
Ben was upset,
Ben was battered every day,
Ben was unwanted,
I take his hand and smile at him,
And he smiles back.

Alwin Saji (8)
Springhill RC Primary School, Southampton

Making The World A Better Place

Jake upset, unwanted every day,
Jake beaten and battered every day,
Jake unhappy and unloved every day,
Always a black cloud follows him,
I put my hand on his shoulder,
I pick him up and smile at him,
I say 'Don't hide, come with me,
I will look after you.'
The cloud disappears and the sun shines on both of us,
'Thank you,' whispered Jake.

Franz Lophanor, Samuel Ricaud & Mateusz Szwec (7)
Springhill RC Primary School, Southampton

Making The World A Better Place

Ella, lonely every day,
Ella, beaten every day,
Ella, unwanted every day,
Ella, sad every day,
Ella, hated every day,
Ella, attacked every day,
Ella, left out every day,
Ella, unloved every day.

Feeling alone and small,
I take her hand and smile,
She smiles back,
The black cloud disappears
And the sun shines.

Elliott Connelly & Mateusz Swiekatowski (7), Klaudia Sugier, Thany Mguni, Jake Jones, Dominic Stasiak & Daniel Hiscock
Springhill RC Primary School, Southampton

Ending Racism

Every day Yasmin walks to school,
Knowing the girls and boys are going to tease and taunt her.

At playtime, she hides behind the oak tree and
Crouches down into a tiny ball with a black cloud around her.

I take her hand and I say, 'Don't hide, come and play with me,'
And the black cloud disappeared and
A lovely happy cloud took its place.

Daisy McKay (7)
Springhill RC Primary School, Southampton

Recycle

R ecycle your paper, your cans, all your trash,
E mpty glass bottles in bottle banks, *smash!*
C ardboard and paper reused, saves the trees,
Y ou must help our planet, do your bit please,
C ompost old food, it helps, can't you see?
L et us remember how our world ought to be,
E veryone help, be aware and remember,
Reduce,
Reuse,
Recycle.

Class of 3MW (7-8)
Springhill RC Primary School, Southampton

Trapped

Extinction is bad,
It's making the panda sad!
He's been put in a circus zoo with no bamboo!
Ears are dropping from his eyes,
As he softly cries,
Help!

Amber McLean & Swaiyaa (10)
Springhill RC Primary School, Southampton

Tigers And Cheetahs

Tigers have stripes,
But they sometimes bite,
Soft and cuddly,
They're so lovely,
Cute and neat,
They look so sweet,
Tears drop from their eyes,
While they slowly drift away and die.

Cheetahs have spots but they get so hot,
They chase and play and run all day,
They run and jump to catch their prey,
But they'll soon fade away!

Ishita Verma, Amy Ward & Zara Jennings (10)
Springhill RC Primary School, Southampton

Don't Litter!

Save the world,
Save it now,
Don't scatter litter,
Not never, not now,
Whatever weather,
Does not mean,
You cannot recycle your litter.

When you've done that,
Everything will be better
For you and for me,
As long as you don't litter,
You'll see!

Gabby Elsden & Heaven Apellido (10)
Springhill RC Primary School, Southampton

The Help Us Letter

Bang! Crash! Down go the trees,
Poor old orang-utan no more leaves,
He's all on his own,
No one by his side,
Save all the forests,
We need your *help!*

Creak! Splash! Down goes the ice,
Poor old polar bear he's on his side,
A broken leg and a bleeding eye,
Floating off towards the horizon line,
Now save the ice,
We must have your *help!*

Aoife Scully (10)
Springhill RC Primary School, Southampton

Poverty

P eople are crying,
O ur animals dying,
V ery much searching for love,
E ntering Heaven thinking *lucky you,*
R escue them now,
T hey need someone's help,
Y ou are the people who they can rely on.

Daisy Marie Walsh (10)
Springhill RC Primary School, Southampton

Poverty!

P eople are out there scavenging for food in dustbins
and wasteland,
O ver hungry children lie in the family bed as Mum
tries to soothe the pain,
V igorous gunfire constantly flying over the innocent village,
E very morning, children cross fields and valleys for a small drink,
R ationed food from rubbish heaps and dirty water is
all the town have,
T hink about it, people can die or lead a very miserable
life due to poverty,
Y ou can make a difference!

Anthony Wood (10)
Springhill RC Primary School, Southampton

War Is Bad

W ar rages, destroying nature,
A nd people are dying in horrible battle,
R ed blood covers the ground.

I n battles animals die,
S adly the whole world changes.

B lasting bombs fly through the air,
A iming for their destiny,
D estroying the whole world without a care.

Joseph Greene (11) & Andzejs Krauklis
Springhill RC Primary School, Southampton

War's Bad

W ar is bad although it goes on,
A nd their skin is bloody from the big bomb,
R ed blood is blanketed over the battlefield,
'S hall we remember those who were killed?

B lasting guns, endless screams,
A nd dead bodies lying in the streams,
D o you want to make a difference?

Callum Thomas (11)
Springhill RC Primary School, Southampton

God's Dream

Wouldn't it be great if countries didn't have wars,
But helped each other more?
People of the world respecting each other.
Everyone sharing together.
Wouldn't it be great if people stopped dropping litter
And everyone tried to get fitter?
Everyone could walk instead of driving a car,
Then the cities would be less smoggy
And we could see the stars.

Blue Group 3JB
Springhill RC Primary School, Southampton

God's Dream

Wouldn't it be great if fighting was banned
And we cared for the land?

Wouldn't it be great if we cared for each other,
Our pets and wild animals, our fathers and mothers.

I love my world.

Jacob Gooding (8)
Springhill RC Primary School, Southampton

God's Dream

Wouldn't it be great if everyone stopped polluting?
Wouldn't it be great if killing was banned?
Wouldn't it be great if everyone loved one another?
Wouldn't it be great if people stopped mistreating the environment?
Wouldn't it be great if my dream came true.

Caitlin Madden (8)
Springhill RC Primary School, Southampton

God's Dream

Wouldn't it be great if people would stop polluting?
I don't think they know what they're doing!
If everyone keeps on polluting, animals will keep on dying,
But people, keep on trying,
Wouldn't it be great if guns were banned
And the world was a better place?

I love my planet.

Jordan Sebuliba Kibbuka (7)
Springhill RC Primary School, Southampton

Violated Earth

Violated Earth,
Sitting polluted alone,
Poisoning the air.

Cruelty kills fish,
Damaged carrier bags float
And hover for life.

Earth needs space for care,
The Earth is not a dumpster,
Treat the Earth wisely.

Litter fills the gaps,
The gaps of the loving Earth,
Covered by rubbish.

Liam Leaves (10)
Westover Primary School, Copnor

Save The Earth

Save the Earth, don't drop,
Sapphire blue sea now ruined,
Stop, think, do not drop,
Cute leatherback turtle dead,
Drifting down the sea,
Gone from the face of the Earth,
Killed by plastic bags,
Together we can do it,
Will you save the turtle?

George Vernon (9)
Westover Primary School, Copnor

Life On The Streets

If you're sad,
If you're poor,
Come on then, knock on the door,
We will give you a bed,
You will get fed,
That's what I said.

If you want a place to stay,
If your children want a place to play,
Then come on down
And we will turn that frown upside down.

Daniel Lopez (10)
Westover Primary School, Copnor

The World

What if the world changed and turned upside down?
Like global warming, cutting down nature;
Well that's happening now!
Help!
What if you just chucked litter and didn't care
And eventually the land was covered and you thought it wasn't fair?
How can we stop that?
Rainforests are going one by one!
What about the animals?
What about the tigers, baboons and bats?
You've torn the world! We're going to be done!

Sophia Truesdell (8)
Westover Primary School, Copnor

What If?

What if the place was tidy?
What if the place was clear?
What if we kept it spotless?
What if everyone wasn't so mean?

What if we didn't waste?
What if we didn't have the environment?
What if we wasted the whole place?
It wouldn't be enjoyment.

What if people dropped their litter?
What if you could help, please now if you may,
If you could, we would love you to,
What if you could help today?

Alastair Thompson (9)
Westover Primary School, Copnor

The Rainforest

There is the rainforest,
Great and tall,
With moisty, wet air,
To cower it all.

There is the crocodile,
Waiting for times long,
See him lying in the sun,
His massive jaws, big and strong.

There is the tarantula,
With his hairy legs,
His poison red back,
Catching flies in his webs.

There is the orangu-tan,
With her golden fur,
Swinging through the trees
And a voice to be heard.

There is the man,
In his hands is the forest's fate,
With his gun of fire
And his sword of hate.

The crocodile, the tarantula
And the orangu-tan flee in fear,
The man's mind is set on destruction,
His eyes shed no tears.

The rainforest is an amazing place,
Its beauty second to none,
'So where is this wondrous place?' you ask,
The answer to that is . . .

Gone!

Carmela Silva-Mason (11)
Westover Primary School, Copnor

Extinction In The Rainforest

The rainforest is dying out,
So are the innocent animals,
All the orangu-tans,
All the gorillas,
On the edge of extinction,
When the future comes,
Brand new unknown technology,
Will cover up the countryside,
All this wonderful nature will die,
Without the trees of the forest,
The soft soil does not survive,
The land becomes a desert
And the creatures of the countryside,
Lose their happy homes,
The monkeys will die like dinosaurs,
The tigers will be killed
With the same speed at which they run.

Alex Sandiford (10)
Westover Primary School, Copnor

Being Homeless Is Very Sad

Being homeless is not much fun,
I wish I could do something but I can't,
People are as scruffy as dogs,
I wish I could save the world,
People crying on the streets,
I see mums crying with their babies,
People smell of smoke,
I don't like seeing animals in the streets,
Especially dogs, I love dogs, but not on streets,
If I saw a puppy on the street, I would cry my eyes out,
I would make a puddle,
I want to take them home with me but I can't,
I really want to save the world.

Steven Andrew Jones (9)
Westover Primary School, Copnor

Recycle Your Rubbish

Hey you! Recycle that, don't throw it in the bin,
Hey you! Recycle that, don't throw it in the sea.

Hey you! Don't chop that tree down, just for paper,
Hey you! An animal lived there.

This place I live in is terrible,
Oh please don't leave me all alone,
Pollution here, pollution there,
Trees falling everywhere.

This isn't a job for one or two,
So come on, do what you can,
Just save a tiny piece of land.

Evie Minker (9)
Westover Primary School, Copnor

What's Happening To Our World?

People crying on the street,
Sleeping on the benches,
Staying in our B&Bs,
With only one room to live in.

Feeling ill with no medicine,
Is a very, very bad thing,
No money to pay for medication,
When with an awful disease.

Losing lots of weight,
Getting thinner and thinner,
Nothing to eat or drink,
Except all the litter.

No doctor to go and see,
Children just have to wait and die,
Their parents call for help
And eventually start to cry.

This is what is happening in our world!

Morgan Taylor (10)
Westover Primary School, Copnor

Do Your Own Little Bit

Chop, chop, down they go,
Down to the ground below.

Splash, splash, pick up that tin,
Think about what lives within.

Broom, broom, down they go,
Couldn't you go slow?

Crash, crash, that was a home
And you destroyed it. Oh no!

Bang, bang, what was that sound?
Oh yeah it was a bird falling to the ground.

So we all know we've got to work for it,
Now we've got to do our own bit.

Isabella Hart (10)
Westover Primary School, Copnor

A Global Warning!

When the Earth was young and the grass was green,
The planet wasn't dirty, it was clean,
There was no gas in the air or oil in the sea,
But the sky was clear, Earth was happy.
Fumes in the air as you sit by the sea,
That horrid thought shouldn't be,
But it will come true, quick! Pick up your litter, that's what to do,
There are dust-filled lands miles long,
Oh why can't the trees come back where they belong?
If icebergs crack because of the hole in the sky,
They will all melt down and we will all drown,
Temperatures will soar, seas will rise,
Take notice of my words - they are wise,
If rainforests disappear and plants die,
The sun will burn through and we will fry,
Cracked, scored lands are all that remains,
This is what we have done, but it could change.

Aaron Lloyd (10)
Westover Primary School, Copnor

Our World

Depressed souls cram the vicious world
And poverty is at every corner you turn,
Behind closed doors starvation is the key
To a dark hole of dismal despair and unhappiness.
Arguments are shouted all over the world,
With religions rebelling against each other,
It's a disgrace that people are judged by the colour of their skin,
Decrepit walkways stretch along the lengthy boulevards
Which are filled with dejected and apprehensive people.

George Parker (10)
Westover Primary School, Copnor

Untitled

Please don't litter, it's not fair,
Because pollution could fly in the air,
Definitely don't throw cans in the sea,
Because I'm sure we can do a good deed.
Don't litter or places will look like a lump of a dump.
Save the environment, don't be scared,
Or pollution will keep getting to your head,
If you keep the world smart,
What you've done could be a work of art,
Don't be mean,
Help me be clean,
If you litter, everything will be bitter and
You will never eat food again,
People who litter are like a dice,
You gamble if you litter or not,
If you help me, you are nice
And you will not see litter in your sight.

Samuel Smith (8)
Westover Primary School, Copnor

What If?

What if the rainforest completely disappeared?
What would happen to rainbow-coloured birds?
What if giant gorillas were only found in zoos?
If only people stopped purposely killing animals,
What if tigers were shot for their coats
That flash like gold in the sunlight?
Why are people destroying the wonderful world we live in?

What if the world came to an end?

Amy Mitchell (8)
Westover Primary School, Copnor

What If?

What if the rubbish kept piling up?
What if it would never stop?

I don't know,
I don't know.

What if all the rainforests were cut down forever?
What if the beautiful animals and perfect life around us
Never breathed again?

I do care,
I do care.

Owen Cook
Westover Primary School, Copnor

Don't!

Don't drop litter, just be helpful,
Don't make our lives really dreadful.

Don't, you're mad, why drop litter?
Don't, just recycle, you'll make the world better.

Don't just sit there, make things better,
You could be an example setter.

Just recycle, I said it before,
Please don't start a litter war!

Please!

Kayleigh Smith (9)
Westover Primary School, Copnor

Our Friend Earth

Our friend Earth,
Is blue and green,
She makes a home,
For you and me.

But down on the ground,
There is something going round,
Air pollution,
Is destroying the world.

We should stop it,
By reducing our carbon footprint
And switching things off,
Not leaving them on standby.

So if we do that,
Our friend Earth,
Will be great
And will give birth to everyone.

Jamie Fisher (8)
Westover Primary School, Copnor

Young Writers Information

We hope you have enjoyed reading this book - and that you will continue to enjoy it in the coming years.

If you like reading and writing poetry drop us a line, or give us a call, and we'll send you a free information pack.

Alternatively if you would like to order further copies of this book or any of our other titles, then please give us a call or log onto our website at www.youngwriters.co.uk

Young Writers Information
Remus House
Coltsfoot Drive
Peterborough
PE2 9JX
(01733) 890066